THE 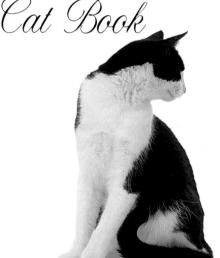 LITTLE
BLACK
Cat Book

D A V I D   T A Y L O R

D A P H N E   N E G U S
Consulting Editor

SIMON AND SCHUSTER
New York • London • Toronto • Sydney • Tokyo • Singapore

A DORLING KINDERSLEY BOOK

SIMON AND SCHUSTER

Simon & Schuster Building
Rockefeller Center
1230 Avenue of the Americas
New York, New York 10020

Simultaneously published in Great Britain
by Dorling Kindersley Limited,
9 Henrietta Street, London WC2E 8PS

PROJECT EDITOR Corinne Hall
PROJECT ART EDITOR Nigel Hazle
MANAGING ART EDITOR Nick Harris
MANAGING EDITOR Vicky Davenport

Printed in Italy by Mondadori

1   3   5   7   9   10   8   6   4   2

Library of Congress Catalog Card Number: 90-32245 [tk]
ISBN: 0 - 671 - 70984 - 4

C O N T E N T S

CREATIVE
Cats

*The black cat as
inspiration in the art,
literature and mythology
of all ages, the whole
world over.*

FANTASY AND FOLKLORE

Black cats have featured in myths and stories for thousands of years. Here are some fascinating examples.

Between medieval times and the seventeenth century, black cats were feared and hated all over Europe. Their sinister appearance gave rise to the belief that they were the Devil's familiars. Woe betide any old lady who befriended a black cat, for she would soon find herself burned alive as a witch, alongside her feline familiar.

LUCKY FOR SOME

Gradually this fear diminished, and it was then thought instead that to have a black cat in the household would keep the Devil at a respectful distance. In some areas it was considered lucky to meet a black cat accidentally. And if one walked deliberately across your path, this was usually regarded as a good omen.

The luck could be reinforced by stroking puss three times. In some places, it was believed that the luck was lost if the black cat then crossed from left to right, turned back on its tracks or ran away from the person who first saw it.

LUCKY IN LOVE

Black cats are always welcome at weddings. If a black cat crosses the path of the couple as they leave the church, happiness is guaranteed. There is an old saying: "Wherever the cat of the house be black, the lasses of lovers will have no lack." And one of Rudyard Kipling's *Just So Stories* tells the tale of the independent "Cat that Walked By Himself" that refused to submit to human domination.

BLACK VERSE

This well-loved nursery rhyme
first appeared in print in 1765:
Hey, diddle diddle,
The cat and the fiddle,
The cow jumped over the moon.
The little dog laughed to see such
sport,
And the dish ran away with the
spoon.

Left: The Cat and the Fiddle;
Top: Feline Familiar;
Right: Kipling's Independent Puss

AMAZING BLACK-CAT FACTS

Cats are a subject of fascination to nearly everyone. Here are some tantalizing black-cat facts to delight cat lovers.

More superstitions are attached to black cats than to any other feline type. In many countries they are symbols of good luck - although not in America, Italy or Portugal, where white cats bring good fortune; or China, where black is a portent of ill health or poverty. Perhaps it is the black cat's mysterious qualities that inspire such great and lasting devotion from its owners. Two of the richest bequests ever made to animals were given to black cats.

FORTUNATE FELINES

One such cat was named Pussy. She was a comfort to Mrs Dorothy Walker during the reclusive widow's last few months, giving her great companionship and lasting consolation.

As a token of her gratitude, she left her entire fortune of around $6 million to an animal charity, on condition that they took the greatest care of Pussy for the rest of her life. Another treasured pet, Blackie was bequeathed an entire house for his exclusive use when his devoted owner sadly died.

WORKING CATS

The mouse population at the Home Office in London was kept under strict control by a black male cat. The last mouser to be put on the payroll broke the tradition by being female. Peta was a black Manx cat and had a territory of 200 rooms and miles of corridor to patrol until she retired.

BLACK LOOKS

One black Persian cat who did nothing for his keep except look remarkably beautiful was Dirty Dick. Fourteen times overall champion in the early 1900s, his only other task in life was to father the next generation of pretty, prize-winning kittens.

Far Left:
Fastidious
Feline;
Above Left:
Tactile Cat;
Right:
Cuddlesome
Cat.

HALL OF FELINE FAME

Here are some black cats that have graced the corridors of feline fame in history, film and advertising.

Black cats often have sinister roles to play in films. *Cat People* and *The Curse of the Cat People* tell the story of a brother and sister who could turn themselves into ferocious panther-like cats. Black cats perform to chilling effect in several cinema versions of *The Black Cat*, each loosely based on the Edgar Allan Poe story in which a murderer's crime is revealed by the cat he loathes.

CARTOON CAT

A cozier, more comfortable black cat, Felix by name, starred in the first cartoon ever made with sound in 1930. The American public adored his antics, and his popularity was such that Felix drew audiences larger than Charlie Chaplin or Buster Keaton.

The age-old rivalry of cat versus bird was the theme of the Sylvester and Tweety-Pie cartoons. Tweety, smug singer of the immortal lines "I tawt I taw a puddy tat," drove Sylvester to increasingly manic, and inevitably unsuccessful, attempts to finish off the canny canary once and for all

BLACK MAGIC

A connection with good luck and magic made black cats an obvious subject for birthday and greeting cards. Black cats were also an extremely popular advertising logo used to promote everything from elegant *Craven A* cigarettes to all varieties of chocolate, nylon stockings, fabric dyes and stove polish.

Left: Felix thinks: "I'd go through fire and water for her, but I'd sooner be nearer the fire!" Right: Midnight Feast with a Cat of Midnight Black. Below Right: Black Doorstep Cat.

WORK ASSOCIATES

Raymond Chandler and his black Persian, Taki, featured on the covers of the author's books in the 1940s and 1950s. Taki would sit on his owner's manuscript and assist with revisions while the author worked. And, on a more sinister note, Richelieu, French statesman and cardinal, kept a firm and controlling hand on affairs of state with the help of his black Angora cat, Ludovic the Cruel. Ludovic would sit regally on the senior statesman's lap, keeping him company as he signed the day's death warrants. It must have been a sinister sight to behold!

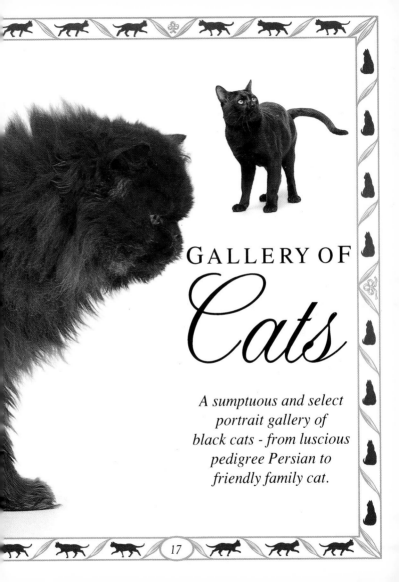

GALLERY OF
Cats

*A sumptuous and select
portrait gallery of
black cats - from luscious
pedigree Persian to
friendly family cat.*

FELINE FEATURES

Every cat's features are uniquely expressive of its innermost character. Breeding often shows itself most obviously in the face, and especially in the eyes, the windows of the soul, which are also monitors of the slightest changes in mood, health or well-being. An alert, sparkling, interested cat is a joy to behold, as any cat lover will agree.

BELUGA
Black Persian

BOBBIE
British Black Shorthair

JANCIS
Bombay

PETERKINS
Bicolor Persian

GEORGIE
Non-pedigree

TIGGY
Non-pedigree

COY
Non-pedigree

BONNIE
Non-pedigree

THE BOMBAY

The Bombay's superb coat puts it in a black-cat class all its own. Coal black from root to tip, the fur is dense, silky and as glossy as patent leather. These cats are named after the Indian city of Bombay because they look like minute Indian black leopards. Most common in America, the pedigree was created here in the 1950s.

*E*XOTIC FOREBEARS
The beautiful Bombay is a cross between the American Black Shorthair and the enchanting Burmese, from which it gets both its satin-soft, lustrous coat and its affectionate nature.

*E*YES *A*S *B*IG *A*S *S*AUCERS

The huge, wide-set eyes of the Bombay range in color from brilliant ocher to deepest copper, and make a striking contrast to its gleaming, pitch-black fur.

*T*HE *P*URR-FECT *C*ITY *C*AT

Bombays are ideal apartment-dwelling cats because they don't mind in the least if they cannot roam too much outdoors.

They are delightfully sociable creatures, however, and must not be left alone for long.

*C*ATERISTICS

Playful and extremely friendly, loves people and company.

Gets lonesome if left alone for too long.

Won't roam much from home.

BICOLOR PERSIAN

The original standard for breeding the Bicolor was intended to produce a cat with markings like a Dutch rabbit: a minimum of white feet, legs, underside, chest and muzzle. An inverted "V" blaze on the face is desirable. Breeders found this so difficult to achieve that the regulations were modified. Now, Bicolors can have random, even patching. This is the ultimate designer cat!

*P*RETTY *F*ACE
The ears are small and neat, with long tufts. A blaze on the face, shaped like an inverted triangle, is a sought-after feature.

Astonished
Prominent white eyebrows give this fluffy little rascal a permanently surprised expression.

Cateristics
❧

Docile and loving.
❧

A perfect household pet.
❧

Adorably cuddly and cute.

Different Theme
An unusual variation is the Van Bicolor which has a white body with patches of color on the tail and head. One, or at most two, patches are allowed on the body.

BLACK PERSIAN

Who could resist this adorably fluffy cat, with its glistening golden eyes? One of the first breeds to be recognized, perfect specimens remain a rarity. The problem lies in producing a coat that is blacker than black: no trace of markings or stray white hairs are permitted in the fully grown Black Persian. This cat needs careful cosseting and regular grooming to keep its splendid coat in tip-top condition.

PAWS FOR EFFECT
Even the large, round paws and pretty nose are black on this cat: those luminous amber eyes are the only contrast.

PRIZED PUSS
Voted Cat of the Year a record-breaking three times in America, these show cats are forced to lead sheltered lives: too much damp can make a prize-winning coat look "rusty"; too much sun, and it begins to lighten.

R<small>UFF</small>

The Black Persian wears a handsome ruff of black fur around its neck which frames a broad face with the snub nose characteristic of Persian cats.

C<small>ATERISTICS</small>

🐈

Very loving to its nearest and dearest.

🐈

Extremely responsive to pampering.

🐈

Loves attention and needs lots of tender loving care.

BLACK BRITISH SHORTHAIR

As a kitten, the Black British Shorthair is permitted to show faint traces of tabby markings, or even a coppery tinge that may deepen if the cat spends too long in the sun. But by the time the cat is about six months old, it must be blacker than black, the fur evenly colored from root to tip, with no rusty tinge, or stray white hairs. A perfect specimen is a rarity to be treasured.

GLITTERING GOLD
Vivid, sparkling golden eyes give this cat's breeding away: very different from the green eyes of the non-pedigree black cat.

PRIZED FEATURES

A prize-winning Black British must look like a shadow, dark as night - even the whiskers should be black, not to mention the cat's nose and paw pads.

WELL-BRED

A coal-black kitten may make an appearance in the litter of a tortoiseshell mother. More often these cats are produced by mating two British Blacks.

CATERISTICS

🐈

Loves attention and affection.

🐈

An affable nature.

🐈

A quick, lively intelligence.

GEORGIE

Georgie's owner dropped into the pet store one day to buy a can of dog food for a friend - and came back with an irresistibly fluffy black kitten. That was how Georgie - her name is short for Georgina - found her home, and she has been sharing it happily with three pedigree cats ever since. Her special friend is a White-gloved Birman. The two love to sit side by side, hugging each other.

N EAT EATER

Georgie is not a greedy cat, but she adores evaporated milk, and has to have her own special brand of cookies to keep her happy.

WATER-BABY

One way to keep Georgie amused is to turn on the garden hose. She is fascinated by water, and will spend hours trying to catch the drops.

PLAY-TIME

Georgie's favorite toy is a home-made mouse that gets a thorough paw-pounding whenever she wants to play a game or two.

CATERISTICS

Pretends to be a stuffed cat by sitting very still on the top of the kitchen cupboard!

A model of good behavior.

Eats little and often, never over-indulging.

TIGGY

Meet Tiggy, the talking cat! If he's not purring - and he usually is - Tiggy is talking to his owner. They have many long conversations, and Tiggy responds to anything that's said to him with a polite "Meow!" He has different tones of voice to indicate that he's hungry, in need of a hug, or just feels like passing the time of day. He follows his owner from room to room, purring loudly to let her know he's there.

PLAYFUL PUSS
Tiggy's favorite game is chasing anything that moves: falling leaves, the vacuum cleaner or, best of all, the cat next door.

PURR-FECT GIFT

When Tiggy was a tiny kitten, he was given to his owner as a surprise present from her daughter - one of the best gifts she has ever received.

CATERISTICS

🐈

Will eat crab, sardines or chicken with very little persuasion.

🐈

A placid cat, with a very sweet nature.

🐈

Sleeps on the bed when he gets the chance - the sofa is second best!

ATTENTION-GRABBING

If no one hears Tiggy when he scratches at the door, he presses his face against the window, meowing loudly until someone notices the noise and lets him in.

COY

Black-and-white cats have been a familiar sight in farmyards for centuries. Coy was born on a farm and spends his days enjoying the freedom of a life in the country. But farm cats are expected to do a bit of work for their living, and Coy makes sure that he catches his fair share of mice around the barns and stables. His life is not too hard, however, and he is allowed into the farmhouse after dark to sleep in a blanket-lined basket in front of the fire.

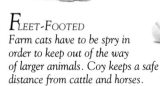

*F*LEET-FOOTED
Farm cats have to be spry in order to keep out of the way of larger animals. Coy keeps a safe distance from cattle and horses.

CATERISTICS

🐾

*Keeps his white tummy
and pink paws
scrupulously clean.*

🐾

*Enjoys catnapping,
keeping one eye open.*

🐾

*Good at scrambling up
trees - and knows how
to get down again!*

WELL FED

*Although Coy supplements his diet with
freshly caught mice, he is not expected to
hunt in order to survive, and is given two
good meals a day by his owners.*

SNOOZING SPOT

*Coy keeps a watchful eye on his
domain from a favorite perch, on
top of a sunny wall near the pigsty.*

BONNIE

 Bonnie is so lovable, it is difficult to believe anyone could neglect her - yet when her present owner rescued her, she was an undernourished kitten. Bonnie hasn't looked back since. Fifteen years on, contented and middle-aged, she loves spending time snoozing between meals. Her days have not always been so uneventful: at one time, she disappeared completely from home, reappearing unharmed and happy seven weeks later, to her owner's great relief.

COMPLETELY SPOILED

Bonnie cannot resist a piece of fresh fish, and enjoys turkey, cooked especially for the lucky feline residents to share.

FULL HOUSE

Bonnie shares a home with her sister Charlie,
brother Caspar and fifteen pure-bred Burmese.
Generally, all the cats get on very well.

CATERISTICS

❧

Always sleeps in the coziest
spot on offer.

❧

Loves catnip mice!

❧

Adventurous in the past,
but too lazy to take many
risks these days.

FRIENDLY FELINE

An exceptionally sociable cat, Bonnie once won
the Friendliest Pussy-Cat Prize at her local show.
Her idea of heaven is a warm lap to sleep on.

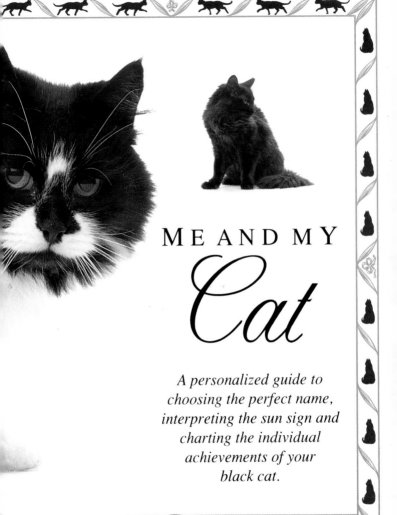

ME AND MY
Cat

A personalized guide to choosing the perfect name, interpreting the sun sign and charting the individual achievements of your black cat.

My Cat's Purr-sonal History

My cat's name ....

Date of birth ....

Birthplace ....

Weight ....

Sun sign ....

Color of eyes ....

Color of coat ....

Distinguishing features..

Mother and father (if known) ....

Brothers and sisters ....

My Cat's Favorite Things

Gastronomic goodies ....

Napping spots ....

Cat-tricks and games..

Special stroking zones...

Main scratching post ....

THE FIRST TIME MY CAT...

Opened its eyes ....

Drank a saucer of milk ....

Ate solid food...

Sat on my lap and purred ....

Said "Meow!" properly ....

Understood the point of kitty litter ....

Presented its first mouse-gift ....

Got stuck in a tree ....

Tried to climb into the bathtub..

Met a strange cat ....

Fell in love ....

Ran up the curtains ....

Saw a dog ....

Smelled catnip ....

Used body language ....

Used the cat-flap ....

Went exploring outdoors..

NAMES AND NAMING

"The Naming of Cats is a difficult matter," wrote T. S. Eliot in *Old Possum's Book of Practical Cats*. He didn't make it any easier by suggesting that cats should have "three different names": one "the family use daily", one that's "more dignified", and one known only to the cat, a "deep and inscrutable, singular Name". Nevertheless, the following suggestions may solve the problem for you!

AUBREY *After the dissolute artist Aubrey Beardsley, who featured black cats in his striking illustrations.*

BLACKBERRY *A pretty name for a puss that's plump as a ripened fruit.*

BOOTS *For a cat with glossy black paws.*

BUSTOPHER JONES *T. S. Eliot's "cat we all greet as he walks down the street in his coat of fastidious black". He is remarkably fat and wears white spats!*

CLEMENTINE *A black cat of this name could often be seen roosting in the organ pipes of an old church in London.*

EBONY *Give this name to a glossy black cat that likes strolling along the piano keyboard.*

FELIX *Cartoon cat-star who rose to fame in the 1920s.*

FREYA *Scandinavian love goddess of mythology who traveled in a chariot drawn by two black cats.*

JET *For a cat with a blacker-than-black shiny coat.*

JOLSON *After Al, singer of "Mammy", for a cat with passion and a big voice.*

KIPLING *Author of the Just So Stories, who illustrated "The Cat that Walked by Himself" with a striking black silhouette of a lone black puss.*

LUCKY *Black cats are said to bring good fortune in many countries - although in some places, including America and China, white cats are the lucky ones, and black cats are reputedly bad omens.*

ODILE *The Black Swan in Swan Lake, enchanted by the magician and endlessly seductive.*

PLUTO *Demon god of the underworld.*

SIBYL *The name means "a sorceress", making it an appropriate name for a witch's familiar.*

Cat Sun Signs

Check out your cat's sun sign and pick a compatible pet.

Aries
March 21 - April 20

Adventurous creatures, Aries cats are not restful pets. Although fiercely independent, they have a very loyal streak, and adore being fussed over when in the right mood. *LIBRAN owners lavish attention on the egocentric Aries cat; AQUARIAN owners like the Aries cat's straightforward approach to life.*

Taurus
April 21 - May 21

The Taurean puss is always purring and is happiest when asleep on its favorite bed. Taureans love food and, not surprisingly, tend to be rather plump. Placid and easy-going, they react fiercely if angered. *VIRGOAN owners create the home Taurean cats love; PISCEAN owners are relaxed by Taurean cats.*

Gemini
May 22 - June 21

An out-and-about cat that gets restless if expected to be a constant, lap-loving companion. An incurable flirt, the Gemini cat's lively nature make for fascinating, sometimes exasperating, company. *SAGITTARIAN owners share the Gemini cat's need for challenge; VIRGOAN owners won't restrict Gemini cats.*

CANCER
JUNE 22 - JULY 22

Ideal for someone who spends a lot of time at home, the Cancer cat will be constantly at your side, climbing on to your lap at every opportunity. But tread carefully: Cancer cats are easily offended. CAPRICORN *owners suit the Cancer cat's desire for stability;* TAUREAN *owners give Cancer cats security.*

LEO
JULY 23 - AUGUST 23

King or queen of the household, Leo cats must rule the roost unchallenged. They have a striking appearance and keep their coats in shape. They adore praise and will go out of their way to attract attention. CANCER *owners like Leo cats taking charge;* ARIAN *owners enjoy the Leo cat's acrobatics.*

VIRGO
AUGUST 24 - SEPTEMBER 22

"Take no risks" is this cat's motto. Intelligent thinkers, Virgoan cats don't mind if their owner is out all day and love a change of scene or a trip in the cat basket. SCORPIO *owners complement the Virgoan cat's inquisitive nature;* GEMINI *owners have an independence Virgoan cats respect and encourage.*

LIBRA
SEPTEMBER 23 - OCTOBER 23

You can't pamper this sensuous feline too much.
Librans crave attention, are quick to take offense
and don't take kindly to being unceremoniously
shooed off a comfy chair. *ARIAN owners are good foil
for tranquil Libran cats; CAPRICORN owners make the
Libran cat feel snug and secure.*

SCORPIO
OCTOBER 24 - NOVEMBER 24

Passionate, magical cats with a magnetic presence.
Leaping and bounding with immense *joie de vivre*,
the Scorpio cat doesn't usually make friends easily
but, once won over, will be your trusty ally for life.
   *PISCEAN owners share the Scorpio cat's insight;
TAUREAN owners entice the Scorpio cat back to base.*

SAGITTARIUS
NOVEMBER 23 - DECEMBER 21

Freedom-loving rovers, Sagittarian cats lack the
grace of other signs. Their great loves in life are
eating and human company, but too much fuss
makes them impatient. *LEO owners like the
Sagittarian cat's brashness; AQUARIAN owners are
intrigued to see what the Sagittarian cat will do next.*

CAPRICORN
DECEMBER 22 - JANUARY 20

Unruffled and serene, Capricorn cats are rather
timid with strangers. They crave affection but may
feel inhibited about demanding it. Be sensitive to
their needs. *CANCER owners like the settled existence
which Capricorn cats love; GEMINI owners offset the
Capricorn cat's tendency to get stuck in a rut.*

AQUARIUS
JANUARY 21 - FEBRUARY 18

Unpredictable, decorative and rather aloof, admire
your Aquarian cat from a distance. Inquisitive, this
cat rarely displays affection for humans, but
observes them with interest. *LIBRAN owners
understand an Aquarian cat's feelings; SAGITTARIAN
owners share the Aquarian cat's unemotional approach.*

PISCES
FEBRUARY 19 - MARCH 20

Home is where the Piscean cat's heart is. The lure
of the garden wall holds no attraction for these cats.
Attention centers on their owners, who can be
assured of a Piscean puss's single-minded devotion.
*LEO owners find Piscean cats entertaining; SCORPIO
owners have a dreaminess Piscean cats find irresistible.*

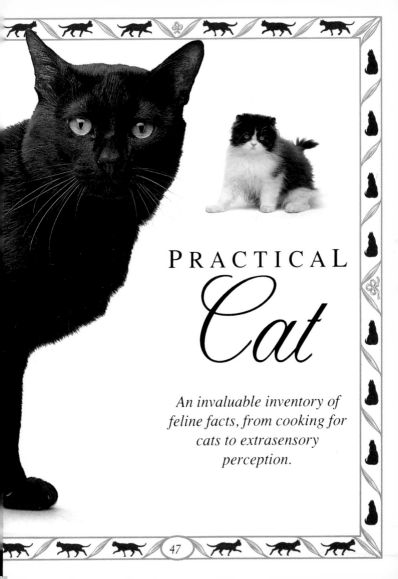

PRACTICAL
Cat

An invaluable inventory of feline facts, from cooking for cats to extrasensory perception.

Choosing a Kitten

Choosing a kitten is great fun - but before your
new friend agrees to move in, she will
want to know the answers to a few questions!

Which Kitten?

Persians are luscious, but do you have
time to spend on grooming? Are you
happy to pamper a pedigree, or do
you want an easy-going cat with
an independent streak? Should
kitty be prepared to spend
time alone? Does neutering
fit in with your ideals, and
if not, can you cope with
the consequences? If
you decide on a
pedigree, go to a
recognized breeder.
For a non-pedigree,
try a cat-rescue
society. It is best to
avoid pet stores.

When you come to choose a kitten, it is wise to bear the following pointers in mind:

1 *Choose the brightest, sassiest kitten of the litter.*

2 *Look for clear eyes, clean ears and nose, sound white teeth and no signs of a tummy upset.*

3 *Make sure the fur is glossy and healthy, with no fleas, skin problems or blemishes.*

4 *Check that your kitten is lively and inquisitive, running and jumping with ease, eager to play.*

5 *Don't take kitty home under ten weeks old.*

6 *Check that necessary vaccinations have been given.*

Homecoming

Bring your kitten home in a sturdy box. Give her lots of love, play with her, and don't rush her if she's shy at first. She'll need a warm bed, a litter tray that's regularly cleaned, and her own bowls for food and water. Let her have a good look round before she meets any other household pets. It may take her a while to feel at home, but you will know she's decided to stay when she leaps on to your lap with a contented purr!

Cute Kitten
Who could resist this adorable ten-week-old kitten?

CAT-CHAT

Cats are consummate communicators. They use every part of the body, with subtle vocal variations, to make themselves understood. Here is a guide to demystifying feline bodytalk.

Tail Talk

- A straight tail with a slight bend at the tip means, "This looks most interesting."
- A tail held stiffly at right-angles to the body means, "Hello. How nice to see you."
- A tail with a tip that twitches means, "I'm starting to get angry!"
- A tail waved vigorously from side to side means, "You're for it!"
- An arched tail with the fur fluffed means, "This is my territory and don't you forget it!"
- A tail held low with fur fluffed out means, "I'm frightened." A terrified cat will crouch down low and the fur will stand on end all over its body.

Tones Of Voice

- Purring can mean, "Mmmmm, that feels wonderful," or, "You're my favourite person." However, cats have been known to purr when in pain or distress.

- A little chirping sound, which mother cats use to marshal their kittens together, is given by adult cats to say "Hi" to their owners.
- Yowling and caterwauling usually mean, "Get off my territory," rather than, "What are you doing tonight, gorgeous?"
- Hissing and spitting mean, "Get off my patch of ground, or else." These noises may have originated with wild cats imitating the sound of an angry snake.

Best Buddies

There is, however, no telling what these two are thinking!

Body Language

- Rubbing the body or head against an object is a way of marking territory. When kitty rubs lovingly round your legs, he is saying, "You're all mine."
- A cat with his ears back flat on to his head is saying, "Help!"
- The cat who greets you by rolling lazily over on to his back, presenting his furry underside for you to admire, is saying, "I feel completely safe with you." Don't be tempted to tickle that fluffy tummy: most cats find the area very sensitive, and are likely to react with a reproving paw-swipe.

- An arched back, with straight legs, wide, staring eyes and electric-shock tail mean, "Back off now, or I'll attack!"

CELEBRATION CUISINE

Tsar Nicholas I of Russia fed his cat, Vashka, a celebratory concoction of the best caviar poached in rich champagne, with finely minced French dormouse, unsalted butter, cream, whipped woodcock's egg and hare's blood. Rather than trouble his servants, Doctor Johnson himself purchased oysters for his cat, Hodge. It's not necessary to go to *quite* these lengths on those special days when you want to lavish a little more affection on your puss, but here are some gastronomic goodies which will tempt the fussiest feline.

KITTY VOL-AU-VENT

Spoon a dainty, puss-sized portion of cooked chicken and creamy sauce into the pastry case. Top with shrimp for extra-special appeal. Full of protein and vitamins.

LIVER AND BACON BONANZA

Top kitty's portion with crumbled cheese and serve warm. Packed with essential vitamins, minerals and proteins, this is a guaranteed gastronomic success.

Puss's Shrimp Cocktail

Fresh shrimps on delicate slivers of brown bread, thinly spread with butter and diced into feline-sized mouthfuls. Elegant and full of energy-giving goodness.

Mackerel Puss Pate

A dessertspoonful of mackerel pâté on fresh fingers of toast makes an instant treat for the fish-loving feline. Rich in protein and Vitamin A.

Rare Treat

Raw steak or ground meat, fresh from the butcher's and finely chopped, is a special occasional food for your cat. But be careful not to overdo the raw meat content of your cat's diet.

Drink To Me Only

Not all cats like drinking milk. Make sure there's always an adequate supply of water for your puss. Or try a tempting sip of evaporated milk, or even milky, lukewarm tea.

Tuna Treat

Tuna, in oil or brine, topped with crumbled cheese and grilled lightly makes a well-balanced, heart-warming feast for your feline.

Sweet Puss

Cats can be partial to cantaloupe, the occasional segment of apple, or even the odd sweet grape. Full of essential, health-giving Vitamin C and dietary fiber.

CAT GLAMOUR

If you are the proud owner of a Persian cat, it's essential to give your pet a daily grooming session. Shorthaired cats are better at looking after their coats, so a good brush-and-comb once or twice a week is all they need.

TOOTH CARE
Check the teeth for tartar build-up and, if necessary, clean with a soft brush and baking soda solution.

GROOMING THE FUR

1 *Work grooming powder into the coat. For best results, always make sure it is evenly distributed.*

2 *Brush the fur upward, all over the body, to remove any trace of tangles and dirt.*

Fur On The Face
This can be brushed gently with a toothbrush, but be careful to stay away from the eye area.

Caring For Eyes And Ears
Clean carefully with Q-tips dipped in a warm, weak baking soda solution.

3 Add the finishing touches by brushing the fur vigorously all over the body.

4 Shorthaired cats can be given extra shine by rubbing the coat over with velvet, silk or chamois.

A-Z OF CAT CARE

A IS FOR ACCIDENT
Laws protecting injured cats vary from state to state. Keep your pet off the street. Indoor cats live longer, safer lives.

B IS FOR BASKET
Useful for traveling, although harder to clean than plastic carriers. Line with paper towels. Do not leave puss inside for too long.

C IS FOR CAT-FLAP
Use only where outdoors is safe. Fit at cat's-belly-height and make sure it can be locked securely.

D IS FOR DOG
Cats tolerate their presence in the same household and can form lasting canine friendships if they are introduced in early kittenhood.

E IS FOR EXERCISE
There is cat furniture for exercising. Cat trees can be built. Cats flex their muscles in boisterous play sessions with their owners. A few can even be trained to walk on a special cat leash.

F IS FOR FLEA COLLAR
Put one on puss every summer, before he starts scratching. Check it fits properly and does not rub.

G IS FOR GRASS
Cats love to eat and regurgitate it, along with any hairballs. Indoor cats should be given a pot-grown clump to graze on.

H IS FOR HANDLING
Most cats adore a cuddle, but pick puss up gently and support his whole weight. Don't grab him by the scruff or hold him under the front legs without a steadying hand under his rear.

I IS FOR ILLNESS AND INJECTIONS

Feline Infectious Enteritis and Pneumonitis are the two big - but preventable - dangers. Have your cat vaccinated at around 12 weeks old and remember to arrange booster shots. Reputable catteries will not accept cats for board without certificates showing proof of vaccination.

J IS FOR JACOBSON'S ORGAN

Cats occasionally make a strange "grimacing" facial expression, with the lip curled back, when specific smells such as catnip waft past. They are making use of Jacobson's Organ, an extremely refined sense of smell which responds delightfully to certain triggers.

K IS FOR KEEPING STILL

Something a cat can do to perfection, but never when you are trying to administer medicine! Liquids or crushed pills can be added to food. Or grasp the cat's head and bend back gently until the mouth opens. Press on each side of the mouth to increase the gap, and pop the medicine on the tongue as far back as you can. Close the mouth firmly until the cat swallows.

L IS FOR LITTER TRAY

Put it in a quiet place. Keep it clean and neat. If not, puss may object and perform elsewhere.

M IS FOR MOVING

Keep kitty under lock and key while the move takes place. When you arrive, let him settle in gradually, a room at a time. Much safer to keep puss inside until you're sure he has settled down.

N IS FOR NEUTERING

Male kittens should be neutered at eight - ten months' old; females spayed at five - eight months' old.

O IS FOR OBEDIENCE

Start young, and be persistent. Say "No" firmly, as you pluck puss off the forbidden chair and he'll soon start to cooperate - at least while you're within eyesight.

P IS FOR POISONOUS PLANTS

Avoid the following: azalea, caladium, dieffenbachia, ivy, laurel, philodendron, poinsettia, solanum capiscastrum, or keep them out of your cat's inquisitive reach.

Q IS FOR QUARANTINE

Holiday romances can have costly consequences, as the holidaymakers who fell for a Portuguese puss found out. The cost of quarantine for six months was more than $2000.

R IS FOR RODENT

Cats hunt for sport rather than for nourishment, so be sure to feed your cat well if you want the local mouse colony decimated - a ravenous cat lacks the energy necessary for pursuing swift-footed rodents.

S IS FOR SAFETY

Home is full of hazards for curious cats. Guard open fires; ban cats from the kitchen when ovens and hotplates are on and store sharp knives safely; unplug electrical appliances where cats might chew the cord; keep upstairs windows closed or inaccessible; lock up household poisons and keep the garage closed; beware when using irons; don't leave plastic bags lying around; tidy up tiny objects.

T IS FOR TOYS

The best are often the simplest: a cork swinging from a string, an empty box to hide in, a ping-pong ball, an old spool of thread, a felt mouse for pouncing practice, an old newspaper to stalk - the list of entertaining playthings is endless!

U IS FOR UNMENTIONABLE HABITS

Unneutered toms create the most pungent of smells when they mark out their territory. Even if your pets are neutered, you may need to discourage local toms from visiting via your cat-flap and leaving their overpowering mark, disturbing your household in the process.

V IS FOR VET

If puss has a prolonged stomach upset, seems lethargic, starts sneezing or coughing, looks rheumy-eyed or shows signs of pain when handled, ignore any protests and whisk him to the vet straight away. Vets can also advise on vaccinations.

W IS FOR WORMS

Most cats suffer now and then. Pills are the answer - your vet can advise on this.

X IS FOR XTRA-SENSORY PERCEPTION

Experts argue that cats have no sixth sense, but anyone who observes a cat bristle in response to something unseen by human eyes will be less convinced.

Y IS FOR YOUTH

Enjoy kitten antics! All too soon they will become self-conscious, and save shadow-stalking for when they think you're not looking at them.

Z IS FOR ZOO

Watch out for the African and European Wild Cats, the closest relatives of the average domestic puss. There is a distinct and uncanny resemblance between a tame, snoozing tabby cat and a slumbering tiger: these and other fearsome breeds, like lions and leopards, feature on a more distant branch of the family tree.

I N D E X

ACKNOWLEDGEMENTS

PAGE 10 Hey, diddle diddle, by Arthur Rackham / Mary Evans Picture Library.

PAGE 11 Halloween (detail), Private Collection / The Bridgeman Art Library;
The Cat That Walked By Himself by Rudyard Kipling / Mary Evans Picture Library.

PAGE 12 Black Cat Washing by William Nicholson / Mary Evans Picture Library.

PAGE 13 The Senses: Touch by Jessie Wilcox Smith / Fine Art Photographic Library Ltd;
Cat and Friend by Montbrun / Mary Evans Picture Library.

PAGE 15 The Bed-Time Supper Party / Fine Art Photographic Library Ltd;
My Hallstadt-Cat (detail) by Ditz / The Bridgeman Art Library.

PHOTOGRAPHY: Dave King   **ILLUSTRATIONS:** Susan Robertson, Stephen Lings, Clive Spong

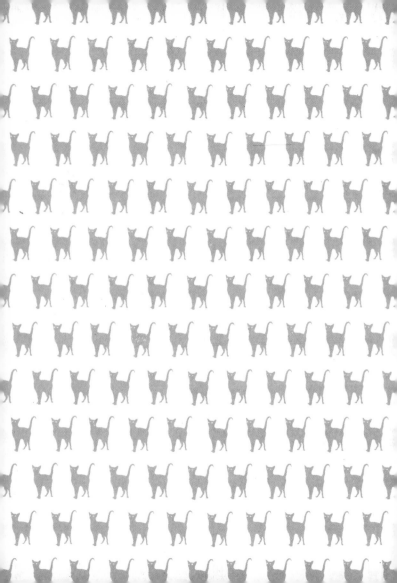